Rejected from the Womb, Accepted by God

Written by LiQuiche L. Young

Rejected from the Womb, Accepted by God
Copyright © LiQuiche L. Young, 2018
Cover image: © Provision Marketing
Back image: © Kingdom's Eye Photography

Published by Chocolate Readings via KDP Publishing
www.chocolatereadings.com

ISBN-13: 9781790885251

Publisher's Note

Table of Contents

A Prayer from the Author

Father God in the name of Jesus, I thank you for your precious people. I pray that you heal every person from rejection that reads this book. I ask that you strengthen their minds, give them rest, and peace in their spirit. There is nothing too hard for you to do. I ask you to fill their thoughts with your thoughts. Guard their hearts; remove the hurtful people from their lives until they're able to stay strong. No weapon form against them shall prosper.

There is no one else like the LORD!!! God you said in your Word, you will never leave or forsake your people. They can do ALL things through Christ that strengthens them.

Your people are accepted by you God because YOU created them. You love your people first. Although they may not understand the journey in life, show them that you created them to love them. Your love is unfailing. Thank you for HEALING in advance.

I ask that you prepare the minds of the readers to receive your healing, understanding, restoration, peace and the gift of forgiveness. We love you, we honor you, and we give you ALL the GLORY and HONOR. In Jesus name I pray. AMEN!!!

Introduction

Rejection: From mother, father, siblings; self-rejection; rejection from the womb. Hurt, deep hurt, wounded, bruised, low self-esteem, anger, bitterness, unforgiveness, lust (a substitute for true love), fantasy lust, harlotry, pride (a compensating spirit for rejection), envy, jealousy, inferiority, insecurity, inadequacy, sadness, grief, sorrow, self-accusation, self-condemnation, depression, hopelessness, despair, despondency, striving, achievement, performance, competition, isolation, selfishness, criticism, covetousness, self-pity, possessiveness, perfectionism, outcast, castaway, black sheep.

Rejection can open the door for a multitude of spirits, including rebellion, pride, bitterness, self-pity, escape, guilt, inferiority, insecurity, fear, hopelessness, fear of judgment, defensiveness, distrust, discouragement, disrespect, hardness, perfectionism, false compassion, false responsibility, material lust, sexual lust, perverseness, self-accusation, compulsive confession, self-promotion, attention-getting, control, withdrawn, fear of love, self-deception, suicide, unworthiness, shame, vanity, unfairness, pouting, unreality, daydreaming, vivid imagination, self-awareness, timidity, shyness, sensitiveness, talkativeness, nervousness, tension, inordinate affection for animals. (Demon Hit List by John Eckhardt)

The questions that run through your head often are: *Why didn't they want me? What did I do that was so wrong? Why can't they love me? Why won't they accept me? Why does my friends and family have their parents and I don't? Why me?*

Have you experienced rejection from family, friends, co-workers, a job, had a failed business, didn't get accepted into a college, failed an exam? If so, then this book is for you too.

After reading this book, you will learn how to identify, overcome and heal from rejection and abandonment. You will learn how to identify toxic relationships and cultivate healthy relationships.

You can't control the environment your parents provided or didn't provide for you; but you can control the outcome. You have the power to let life experiences help you travel to your destiny. Today you have just gone from being rejected from the womb to being accepted by God.

Don't read this book just to read it. Study it, interact with the book, and mediate on the scriptures and things that apply to your life. Put the book down when you feel like you need to and pick it up again. Don't rush through it, take your time. Takes notes in the book, highlight things you want to remember. Have an open heart, open mind and the willingness to receive God's healing for your life. Apply all the knowledge and wisdom to your life and current situations.

Your healing, freedom and acceptance is *today*!! You will no longer accept dark clouds hanging over your life. You will accept everything good that is offered to you. Your life will never be the same again.

You will look at life differently and through a new set of eyes. You will learn how to build yourself up and not tear yourself down, recognize rejection when you see, learn how to control your emotions, have healthy relationships with others and how to let go of the pain and torture of rejection.

It's time to experience life, enjoy life and live on purpose. It's time to live a life that's free and happy with no weights of rejection. Ready or not your life is about to change.

Let's began the journey!

Rejection from the Womb

CHAPTER 1

What is Rejection?

The definition of rejection according to merriam-webster dictionary is: *To refuse to hear, receive, or admit:* <u>REBUFF</u>, <u>REPEL</u> *‹parents who reject their children›*
Obsolete: to cast off

Rejection is when your parent cast you off; their focus is on other things and they abandon you. Rejection walks away and leaves the child for someone else to take care of. Rejection abandons its responsibility and focuses on self. As a child I experienced rejection from my parents. Most of the rejection came from my mother. I experienced rejection in three forms: the womb, emotionally and environmentally.

It Starts in the Womb

Studies show that a child can feel rejected by their parents as early as being formed in the womb. While the womb is an incubator for life, it is also the birth place of rejection. This is the moment when the child feels rejection from their mother.

So, what exactly does it mean to be or feel rejected from the womb? Being rejected from the womb can be an unwanted pregnancy, a contemplated or attempted abortion; maybe the parent didn't want the sex of the child or the child has birth defects/illnesses.

Some mothers may also reject their child in the womb because they are pregnant out of wedlock. The child is considered an illegitimate birth; the mother doesn't want the child and doesn't believe in abortions, so she gives birth from a place of bitterness. These are just a few ways a child can be or feel rejected from the womb.

There are also two type of rejection that a child will experience: emotional and environmental. Let's dive a little deeper into these, and talk about how rejection played a part in my childhood, as well as, adult life.

Emotional Rejection

As a child, I experienced emotional rejection. I felt emotional rejection because I watched my brother being raised by my mother, while I lived with my grandmother. I watched my brother's dad be involved in his life, whereas my dad wasn't around. I watched family members have one or both parents, and I had no parents. I was young and didn't know how to express my emotions. It caused me to be emotionally immature and stopped my emotional growth.

The relationship with my brother and I was great. I enjoyed when he came to my house to visit me. I was very close to my brother as a child. I did, however, noticed that my mother treated us differently. I assumed it was because he lived with her and I didn't. While it stung a little bit, I didn't allow that to stop me from loving him, though. Some children feel rejected if they are compared to their siblings. If the parent shows favoritism with the children or if they have a different mother/father from their siblings, it can make them feel left out. When children grow up in a blended family it's very important for ALL parents to be involved. When a child sees there sibling mother/father active in their sibling's life and their mother/ father isn't active in theirs, it creates a seed of rejection in their emotions.

A child can experience emotional rejection with one or both parents in the home. If a parent is not emotional available for the child it creates rejection.

If their parent suffers from mental illness, if you're adopted, abandoned emotionally or if you experienced a death of a parent. Emotional rejection is like cancer. It's painful, it spreads and it attacks you. Emotional rejection changes the direction and position of feeling loved to feeling not wanted.

Environmental Rejection

When a mother has a child, the child is supposed to be in a safe environment. The safe environment is the home of the mother and father. So what happens when the child's safe environment is unstable? This type of rejection is the womb of an environment; it is a personal womb in the world of a child. It's a womb you can see. It's the place of nurturing and caring. It's the birthing place where a child's growth should feel safe.

As children, we expect our parents to provide a safe place for us, to care for us, love us and teach us. But what happens when your parents can't or won't provide that safe womb for you? What happens if one of your parents has an affair? What happens if your parents get a divorce? The safe place for the child has been altered, changed and reset. The place they knew as safe becomes physically unstable and emotional devastating for the child.

You start experiencing rejection from the physical womb. You feel rejected from the only place you're able to call home. The rejection begins to take root and you have no clue it's rooted. Your safe place is now the most dangerous place in the world, the womb of rejection.

When a child is rejected from a parent it is learned behavior. Do you realize you learned everything as a child from your environment? If you grew up with loving parents, love is what you know. If you grew up with abusive parents, abuse is what you know. If you grew up with parents that are violent, then you know violence. If you grew up with parents that rejected you, you know rejection. Your parents are your foundation of your life. They teach you, mold you and shape you into the adult you have become. The good and the bad is what you become. When you become an adult you have the ability to change and fix some of the learned behaviors you were taught in your environment.

When your parents provided you with instability in your life and emotions, you became a product of your environment. As a child, it's very important to have stability in your foundation. When you don't have a stable foundation, you will have an unstable life.

I had a stable foundation in the home with my grandmother. When my mother came to the home, the environment became unstable. It was unstable because I felt rejected. At one point, I wanted the type of relationship with my mother that she had with my brother. She ignored me a lot and was verbally abusive to me. So when she left my home, order had to be established again. It was ongoing cycle stability, instability back to stability. The environment became confusing. Although it was stable, I had to learn how to go back and forth with the environments provided.

Rejection Produces Fear

Being rejected introduces you to a lot of emotions that are dormant within you. One of the emotions I quickly recognized was fear of being rejected by others. So, before someone could reject me, I rejected myself. I criticized myself before anyone else could. I was my worst critic. I always felt like I couldn't do things right. I was always worried about being judged. Until one day I realized, I didn't need anyone else to judge me because I did it to myself already.

One of the hardest things to do is to tear down the walls you have created around yourself. Not the walls you put up so people won't hurt you, but the walls you created by self-rejection.

Self-rejection is when you cast off yourself, you're abusive to yourself; you reject you before anyone else can reject you. Self-rejection produces low self-esteem, not believing in self, unnecessary worry and identity issues.

People that reject themselves will count themselves out before someone else will. Others will look at it as being negative, but its self-rejection.

Have you ever heard someone say, "I applied for the job, but I know I will never get it." Or they applied for a school, but they say they will never get accepted. Or someone will say you can't achieve that dream and the person agrees.

It's because the person is rejecting themselves and probably don't realize they have rejected themselves because it's their norm. This person most likely grew up in a toxic environment, and haven't identified this issue.

A rejected environment is a toxic environment. The toxic behavior is carried on through environments and words. Being raised in a toxic environment can trigger thoughts and feelings of self-hate. There is nothing worse than hating the person that looks back at you in the mirror.

Check Yourself

Have you said negative words like this before? If so, for the next 24 hours beware of the words you speak. Take a mental note to see if you will speak self-rejecting statements. If you find yourself saying self-rejecting statements, at the end of this book your language will change.

Self-rejection creates a mindset set of worrying. You will begin to worry about what others would say about you. It will also go as far as worrying about situations that may or may not happen. It takes you to a state of mind of *what if.* You're stuck there and you never should have been there in the first place.

Your mind will wonder and think out every negative situation or outcome that's possible. The thoughts will trigger negative emotions and painful memories. Your thought patterns will prepare you to handle situations that will NEVER happen. It will NEVER happen because it's all in your mind. This type of negative behavior will teach you how to reject your thoughts and cause extreme and unnecessary worry and anxiety.

When you're dealing with self-rejection, it will lead you to a road of misery. It will torment you and make you believe things about yourself that isn't true. It's a form of self-destruction. Once you destroy yourself, you and God are the only ones who can piece you back together.

Not only will this behavior torment you, it will cause you not to love yourself, give you a sense of insecurity, and you'll soon lack of confidence.

Rejection Seeks Validation

I must get someone's attention. Why won't anyone pay attention to me? I can't be that bad of a person? Why doesn't anyone want me?

I'm at the point to where I will do anything to be love, accepted, validated, important or popular. Maybe I will join a gang. My gang family will love me.

Or maybe I will become a prostitute. My pimp will protect me.

I will join a sports team; I will join an organization, I need to feel wanted.

I'm just going to accept this abusive relationship this is what love is supposed to feel like right? Who can make me feel special, wanted and love?

My parents never gave me the attention I wanted and needed. I honestly don't even know what I'm looking for.

This is the story of a lot people's lives. It's hard when your foundation was not molded and shaped correctly. You might think what foundation?

The structure of your childhood is your foundation. When a child is neglected and becomes an adult, validation is important. It's important because they never had it. They're trying to find their place in the world and it becomes a struggle.

Broken Women & Validation

A girl's first love should be her father. Her father should show her love, protect her, give her flowers, and tell her she's beautiful, hold her hand, give her hugs and kisses, encourage her, show her stability, support and guide her through life. Pick her up when she falls and wipe her tears when she cries. When a woman gets married and the father gives his daughter away to her husband, he places his daughter's hand into her husband's hands. At that moment he trusts her husband to take care of her just as he did, if not better.

Women usually date men with the same character as their father. This is the example that the father has set. If they date a man lower than the standards the father has set they will disappoint the father and herself.

What happens when you don't have an example of a father? Father's set the foundation of their children's life. Everything you didn't get from your father you look for in other people. You don't know what you're looking for; you're just looking to fill an empty void that you're feeling.

When I started dating I had no clue what I was looking for. I just knew I wanted to be loved. I wanted a man that took care of his children, and I wanted a man that loved his mother. I knew I didn't want a man like my father. My father was an absent father. I found him when I was an adult. He never told me why he wasn't there. Every time I asked he would change the subject.

I always carried the pain of my father being an absent father. I would tell men what I was looking for in the beginning of the relationship. The men would be exactly what I was looking for in the beginning. Somewhere down the line they would change. I couldn't understand why they changed. I stayed longer because I held on to hope. Hoping they would be who they said they were. They told me what I wanted to hear to get what they wanted from me. It left me broken twice.

I got hurt a lot of times because I was looking for men to fill the void my dad created in my life. I dated older men and couldn't understand why. I was looking for a father figure, and not a life partner. I experienced great pain through this process. Although I had a step up dad (step dad) I was still missing something.

It's very important for women to find validation for herself before getting a relationship. From past experiences, I learned looking for validation can be exhausting and draining for yourself, and your partner. When you look for validation and your partner doesn't provide it, you're setting yourself up for disappointment. You must be confident in yourself and learn to valid YOU. You don't need anyone else to do it for you.

CHAPTER 2

The Seed of Rejection

"Whatever you're rooted in becomes your life."

R ejection is often described as refusal, cast off or cast out. It's also known as an inner wound. Inner wounds are not obvious they're hidden. It's not visible to the physical body, but it can be shown in your emotions, actions, and thought pattern.

An inner wound is private. It's something that's intimate, and it's a secret. Sometimes the secret is kept so well you don't even realize it's there. It's a secret within a secret place. This is the place where we experience inner wounds, injured and hurt feelings.

It's a seed that's planted and it grows. For some it's planted at birth, early childhood and even as adults. The seed of rejection grows at different stages of life and also at different paces.

Rejection from the wound simply means to be rejected from the place of creation. It can be in the womb of your mother's stomach, the environment you grew up in, the circle of friends you trust, at work or even family.

The womb is the safe place for you to grow. When you no longer feel safe, wanted or have been injured emotionally, that's when rejection from the womb takes place.

Every person put on this earth wants to experience love. They want to be loved by the people they're surrounded by the most. When the love is no longer there, or love is removed from the safe place, rejection comes.

Rejection is planted like a seed. A seed is planted in the ground. Once a seed is planted in the ground, it must be watered to grow. You can't see the finish product of the tree until it begins to grow.

Once it begins to flourish, you can see the tree growing tall. In the ground is the seed and roots. The roots allow the tree to stand firm, it's hard to destroy a tree.

Once the tree is fully grown it begins to bear fruit. If it's a lemon tree, it will grow lemons. If it's a plum tree, it will grow plums. If it's an apple tree, it will produce apples. If the seed is rejection, the fruit that blooms will not be healthy. Emotions such as apathy, sorrow, rage, and agony, as well as impatience and harshness, being doubtful, bossy, and greedy will begin to grow; causing you to experience a lot of pain and have dysfunctional interactions with the people closest to you. Let's discuss these different types of seeds in depth.

Apathy. This seed causes you to feel indifferent. You might feel like your parent didn't show you enough love. You might feel like your parent loved your siblings more than they loved you. This seed of rejection will continuously replay in your mind like your favorite T.V show.

Sorrow. Sorrow is feeling a deep distress caused by loss or feeling deeply disappointed and misfortune. This seed causes you to feel disappointed every time you think about how you were rejected. Everything around you feels like denial because you felt like your parents didn't love you. You feel like you're safe place is now a place of danger.

Rage, War and Agony. These seeds appear when an outburst of anger and violent behavior leads to destructive behavior. These seeds will cause you to destroy others and yourself. Innocent people will begin to feel the rage that you're feeling. These types of fruit causes someone to transfer their pain and destruction onto others. The behavior is often hostile and unwelcoming. It is an inner violent struggle with prolonged pain and intense or mental suffering. This seed of rejection turns into depression.

Impatience. When this seed blooms into a fruit, the littlest things will affect you in a major way. You no longer have patience towards anything or anyone. You're aggravated, annoyed and short tempered. This seed of rejection can't keep quiet, it must be heard.

Harshness. This is the stage where a person becomes unpleasant in their actions and efforts, ungentle, cruel and bitter. This seed has a double portion. It's physically uncomfortable to be around this person. Everything they say and do is offensive. When they speak, it's as if they are spitting fire and vomiting up all the poison inside of them onto others.

Unbelief and Doubt. When this seed begins to bloom, you're in a state of feeling overwhelmed with fear, indecisiveness, distrust, and in a state of uncertainty, suspense, and confusion. It appears as if people have abandon and rejected you, when in reality they haven't.

Bold, Bossy and Overly Self-Confident. At this stage you're bold and confident in your ignorance. This type of person is so rejected and dejected they're puffed up into self-pride. Their self-pride is so strong it can often be viewed as arrogance. They see no wrong in their behavior and their boldness is displayed in a demeanor that will not allow you to reject them. They boss other people around and don't care if they hurt others in the process. They're inflicting their pain onto to others.

Greed and Intemperance. This is the final seed of rejection. At this stage the person has an aggressive greedy desire. Their desire is strong it must be fulfilled. They don't care how it's done as long as it's done. Their behavior is extreme, intense and it's activated at full speed. Nothing else matters in life besides getting the things they want and their need to feel validated by others. When they feel validated everything is great. Once this feeling goes away they are over whelmed with emotions. Some of the emotions they will feel are hatred, anger, resentment, bitterness, and deep pain. They can't forgive others, themselves, are neglectful, avoids and ignore interaction with others.

The Symptoms of Rejection

Identifying people who are rejected is quite simple. The symptoms of rejection seep out of their spirits. Some sooner than others. What exactly are the symptoms of reject?

- The Silent Treatment
- Walls of Protection
- Depression

- Misplaced Anger
- Insecurity

Let's go into a deep-dive of these symptoms.

The Silent Treatment

What is the silent treatment? The silent treatment is to reframe from speaking to someone. It shows that the person is so hurt they don't have the proper words to express how they feel. The person will experience pain, anger, rejection, abandonment and sometimes rage so they remain silent. It's also known as the silent killer. It destroys you emotionally.

A rejected person will hold all these emotions inside. They will hold it all in because they're suppressing the pain. They can't express themselves properly because they're emotionally immature.

Silence is not how you handle rejection, but this is a common way of handling it. The silent treatment causes division. Silence will teach you to hold it all inside. The more you hold it in, the more pain, fear, and doubt grows. When you function in the silent treatment, you're watering your rejection tree.

Have you ever thought about why when a rejected person gets mad the first thing they do is ignore you? And they will ignore you for long periods of times. They will see you, walk pass you and act like they never met you before. Your existence means absolutely nothing to them. They are functioning from a place of rejection, using the silent treatment. The person that's being ignored usually doesn't even understand what happened or why they're being ignored.

I know this topic very well. I remember growing up as a child, this behavior was normal for me. I adapted to this behavior and this is how I learned how to handle problems and situations. This is the example my mother showed me. I was taught this in my environment. How do I handle this pain I feel inside of being ignored? I felt like I was ready to explode. I was so angry and I couldn't understand why. The pain my mother felt was transferred to me as a child. Why should a child learn how to suppress and not express? They don't. Children do what you do and not what you say.

My mother displayed this behavior most of my life. She would get mad at me and wouldn't speak to me for years. As a child I couldn't understand how you could once have a relationship with someone, and then the next minute it's gone. As if the relationship never meant anything to you.

As a child, I experienced a lot of grief. Not having a relationship with my parents caused a spiritual death within me that I grieved for years. The pain that I endured from my parents neglecting is indescribable.

When a parent walks out of your life, the relationship dies. It's not a physical death, but it causes separation and grieves. God doesn't want you to experience grief and heart breaks. Unfortunately there's no way around this. We all experience these things in some capacity.

Every time I had to separate from someone in life it becomes a grieving process. Can you imagine grieving when someone moves away, dies, separation of friendship and breakups? This was my life.

I learned how to get through this process by using the power of my words. It took me a while to understand this gift, but now I use it when I have to encounter grief on some level. And you can, too.

When God created you, He created you in the image and likeness of Him. God spoke the world into existence with words. He said let there be light and it was light.

You have the power to bring light to the dark places in your life, because you were created in the image and likeness of God. I've learned over the years you can't change anyone, but you can change how you allow someone to treat you. It's always important to pray for others, especially when God instructs you to.

Walls of Protection

Walls of protection are built to guard feelings, avoid disappointment, and to keep one's best interest at heart. This is different from the silent treatment. The silent treatment *shows* pain; the walls of protection *shields* pain.

When a person feels like someone is transferring their pain onto you, it leaves you no choice but to protect them. No one should accept abuse or pain, especially from a parent. Feeling the need to protect one's self causes a person to create a wall.

Has someone ever made you mad before? And after this took place, you decided to forgive them. A few months later they do something else to hurt you. This time it's harder to forgive them. The third time they offended you, now it's hard to let it go. The same behavior keeps repeating itself.

Eventually you will create a wall between you and the person based on their behavior. You need space time to reevaluate the relationship.

You'll need to set some boundaries to teach this person how to treat you.

The boundaries will not be created overnight, it's a process. The wall is built layer by layer, piece by piece and section by section. It takes a series of events to lead up to the walls of protection.

I remember the moment I decided to build a wall of protection from my mother. It was one of the hardest decisions I had to make. The relationship was toxic. Every time we had interaction it wasn't pleasant. I walked away feeling terrible. I prayed and asked God, why should I have a relationship with someone that's toxic to my life, even if it's my mother? I always want to honor my parents, even when they didn't honor me and in their absence. That's what my grandmother taught me.

I felt like I had to honor my mother through communication. A lot people didn't understand my decision to stop communicating with her, and I didn't expect for them to. What people didn't realize is that this situation was bigger than both my mother and I. God approved my choice and that was fine with me.

When God gives you the okay, what others think or feels doesn't matter. The wall was for *my* protection.

It is very important to guard your heart from things and people that will hurt you. You have the power to allow people into your life or release them from your life. *Guard your heart more than anything else, because the source of your life flows from it.* Proverbs 4:23(GWT)

Your heart is the center of who you are. It allows the blood to flow through your body. Your heart is protected by your ribcage. The heart is located directly behind the ribcage. Your heart gives you life. God designed your body so your heart can be protected physically. Isn't it amazing how God places a shield of protection around your heart physically? Now it's up to you to guard your heart spiritually.

I had the hardest time guarding my heart spiritually. I didn't know how to. I didn't know where to start. I was hurt and confused by my past. I was left uncovered and had to learn how to guard myself spiritually and mentally.

Once the heart is tainted, it's a process for it to become pure again. I learn to guard my heart by praying. When I would pray, I really didn't know what to say, so I just prayed. I talk to God as if I was talking to a friend.

It was my beginning and it got me through the process. I asked God to teach me how to pray correctly. I wanted to respect Him and honor Him when I prayed. I wanted to always have a forgiving heart, but I also wanted to guard my heart from unnecessary pain and turmoil.

Guarding your heart more than anything is your job. It's your lifestyle and your protection from evil. It's the place where *you* originate from. It's the place where your peace lives. It's where your faith, your healing and deliverance is received and accepted. Once you receive the joy and abundance of life, it's your job to keep and maintain it.

The wall I built for my mother didn't happen overnight. If you need to build a wall of protection, know that it will take time. Also, know that the wall can be removed at any time.

I have forgiven my mother for all the hurt and pain she has caused over the years. If we could get to a place where we could have a healthy relationship and mutual respect I would knock the wall down.

It's okay to create a wall for your protection. You don't want to walk around like an emotional roller coaster. You don't want to teach the next generation these bad behaviors. In the beginning when you create a wall it might be to heal from all the hurt that was caused from your parent. It's okay to remove yourself from unhealthy environments.

While it's okay to build a wall to restore yourself, it's not okay to create a wall to repay a parent back for all the hurt and pain they have caused you. Only you and God will truly know if this is your intensions.

If you're secretly doing this, you didn't forgive your parent and the work you put into building the wall will be coming from a place of vindictiveness, and that's not healthy. The wall of protection is to create a happy, safe and healthy environment for your life. It is not used to be spiteful, evil or hurtful.

Depression

For many years I struggled with depression. As a Christian, I didn't think I was supposed to struggle from depression. *I believe in Jesus, why was I depressed?* I thought. I noticed the depression got worst. I was trying to pinpoint the root of my sadness. Eventually I realized depression starts with disappointment. I was disappointed by so many things in my life at the time.

I had so many expectations of people and when they didn't meet the expectation I would be disappointed. I didn't make the connection until I started talking to a therapist and reading books on depression.

The littlest things would make me unhappy. I had to learn how to change my thinking. I would get depressed for weeks. I would sit in a dark room. I didn't want to talk to anyone. I would lie in the bed and think about all the disappointments in my life. It would replay in my mind like a recorder. I could clearly see it like a movie in my mind. I would lie down and think about every disappointment I received from my parents over the years.

I would think about my painful past throughout the day, when I took a shower, when I went to bed, day dream about the depression. I was deep in depression and didn't realize how far it was. My mind was in bondage to depression. Depression became my identity, and I identified with it very well. It was my best friend.

I'm thankful that God put trained therapist on earth to help His people with depression. Talking out my issues with a therapist really helped me with my breakthrough.

Some people will never share they struggle with depression. Many people will suffer in silence. You must learn how to identify with what makes you disappointed, teach yourself not to be disappointed and consume your thoughts.

Once you learn *not* to expect things from others, dealing with depression will become easier.

You must figure out what makes you depressed and do your best to avoid them.

One of the things I struggled with was not being understood. When I would express the pain I felt from being rejected from my parents, people didn't understand. It wasn't a big deal to them, but it was a huge deal to me. They would tell me to get over it. When I was told to get over it, I felt rejected from those people. It made me feel like they didn't care that I felt pain. In that moment I experienced rejection twice and it sent me into depression.

I learned that everyone will not understand me and that's okay. I also learned that I can't express myself to everyone. It taught me *not* to look for agreement or validation. When you look for validation and don't get it, it creates frustration and misplaced anger.

Misplaced Anger

When you experience rejection, one of the common emotions is misplaced anger. Anger is defined as a strong feeling of annoyance, displeasure, or hostility. When feeling angry it's common for it to show up in different areas of your life. When you take your anger out on others it's called misplaced anger.

I was very angry as a young adult and I didn't know why. In relationships when I would get mad I remember saying you remind me so much of my father, you remind me so much of my mother. I didn't realize I was holding in anger from my parents.

The rejection and abandonment I experienced as a child carried over into my adult relationships. I remember a relationship I was in; I often told him I didn't like him because he reminded me of my dad.

He would always ask me why I would say that. At that point I didn't know why I would say it, it would just come out. I was still upset with my father for abandoning and rejecting me as a child.

My father raised his step child, but didn't raise me. When I would see other men raise their step children and not their own it would make me upset. I would sit and think, "How could he do that to his child"? I would immediately get mad. I would stay mad for a long time.

I didn't understand this behavior. I needed to know why this made me so upset. I finally learned this was misplaced anger. Misplaced anger is when you're angry at one person and takes it out on another person. It makes you angry every time you think about it, because you never forgave the original offender.

Every time I thought about how my father raised his step children and not raise me it would make me angry. I immediately didn't like a man with these actions. It didn't matter how well I knew them, I would stay away from them. How dare you abandon your child and accept another man's child?

I also found myself thinking about how my mother raised my brother, but didn't raise me. I automatically became an advocate for children. If they were treated unfairly in my presence it would make me upset. I got upset because I had misplaced anger. I felt like the child can't defend its self so I had to defend the child.

I learned how to deal with the root of the anger. I had to write out every single thing my parents did that hurt me and learn how to forgive every single offense. This was the only way to control the misplace anger. You must acknowledge the hurt; forgive the act and the thoughts.

People around you don't deserve to experience misplaced anger. The anger that you feel inside is pushed off onto others. It makes people feel uncomfortable to feel your pain. You must learn how to let go and forgive your parents.

Insecurity

Who am I? Why on earth am I here? Why didn't they love me? I'm not good enough. Why did my life inconvenience my parents? These were my thoughts. These are the thoughts of an insecure person. And at one point I was extremely insecure. Insecurity is struggling to become secure within, not confident, uncertain, uneasy and anxious. And I was definitely all of these things.

For many years I struggled with insecurities. I always felt like I wasn't good enough. I felt like no matter what I did I wasn't enough.

I hated being the center of attention. When all the attention was on me I felt like it was the opportunity for others to find all of my flaws.

In relationships with men I felt like at any time he would leave me. I felt he would reject me and abandon me.

My grandmother raised me in a loving environment, but the thoughts of my parents neglecting me, haunted me. The rejection I experienced from my parents was stronger than the love I received from my grandmother. Unfortunately, the negativity over powered the positive as I became an adult.

Dealing with feelings of insecurity damages an individual. An insecure person will believe thoughts that aren't true; they become anxious for nothing. They're worried about things that may or may not happen. They make things about them when it's not about them. They also struggle with accepting who they are because they haven't discovered their own identity yet.

Being insecure is overwhelming and requires a *lot* of energy. It causes the mind to over think, and it makes you feel like everything is about you, when in reality it's not.

Insecurity will cause you to live in a reality that isn't factual. It's only real to you. An insecure person is constantly looking for validation because they never received validation from the womb of their environment.

My Paralysis Moment

There has been many times in my life that I have felt paralyzed. Not physically, but within. I didn't have the ability to move, act or function because of the life events I experienced. I didn't like the way it felt. I was paralyzed to rejection, anger and abandonment. The pain in my soul just wouldn't go away. I felt tortured.

Moments like this happened *a lot* at night, and when I was alone. I hated being alone because that's when the pain would get intense. I didn't know how to express to anyone how I was feeling so they could understand me. I got to a point that I would hold it all inside. I was afraid of what others might say or think of me. So I didn't share my thoughts.

I read a scripture in the Bible, Mark 2:1-12 NLT, it talks about a paralytic man. He needed to get to Jesus, but it was so crowed. The men that were with the paralytic man were determined to get him to Jesus. They took off the roof of the building to get this man to Jesus. The man was placed on a mat and lowered into the building directly in front of Jesus. What better place to be than in the presence of Jesus.

The paralytic man and the people that helped him, faith was *so* strong. Jesus saw their faith and said, "My child your sins are forgiven." It was if they had a 'by any means necessary' attitude to get him healed. They didn't care what they had to do, they just did it. Jesus saw all of their faith involved. Then Jesus told the paralytic man to stand up, pick up your mat and go home. The man picks up his mat and left. The crowd was all amazed at what they saw.

I have read this story many, many times. But one particular time when I read it, I looked at the scripture differently. I knew I wasn't physically paralyzed, but I know I was paralyzed on the inside. I was desperate to get healed. I wanted to get healed by any means necessary.

I began to go to church more than normal. I was already committed to going to Sunday service and Bible study. The church I attended had two churches; so I had more opportunities to go to church. I found myself at church four days a week. Two nights a week I was in Bible study, I attended prayer on Saturday morning and I attended church service twice on Sundays.

I realize I needed a 'by any means necessary' attitude to receive my healing. I didn't care who was looking at me. I was focused. I had to get rid of all this hurt and pain.

The way I got healed was being in the presence of God. Even when I pulled up to the parking lot I felt God. When people would greet me at the door I felt God's presence, as I sat in my seat waiting for the services to start, I felt God's presence. When the praise and worship team would sing, I felt God's presence. When the pastor spoke the Word of God, I felt God's presence.

The more I went to church, the more I felt the hurt leaving my soul. I continued this pattern for a long time. I knew this would not be an overnight process. I carried this pain for 30 plus years. It will take more than a few weeks to get healed.

I learned that the healing process is a lifestyle change.

I knew where God was and I had to be where He was. The presence of God was at my home, but it's something about worshipping God on one accord with others. The atmosphere was so pure. Anything that was trying to attack me or attach itself to me could not touch me.

I learned how to bring that same atmosphere to my home. I learned how to stay in the presence of God. Throughout this learning process I became free!!! I was no longer bound. I felt brand new on the inside. All the garbage that I carried in my spirit could no longer live there anymore.

After the process was over everyone could see that the Lord was with me. I knew they could see it because many people told me. I went through this by myself. I needed to see that God was with me all along. God said that He is with me. I had to believe it. Even though I felt alone through it all, He showed me He was with me.

It was in the private times of my life when I felt the weakness, but the glory of God was shown on my life. People saw it, when I couldn't see it myself. Being in the presence of God has a way of showing God you accept Him and He accepts you.

When all else failed being in the presence of God helped me; especially on the days I felt weak. I kept showing up and so did God.

When you're feeling broken, lost, and rejected, you must get to God the best way you can. If you have others to help get you there *awesome*!! If not, press your way, crawl, cry etc. Do what you need to do to get out of your paralyzing moment.

Familiar Spirits

When my dad passed away it was the hardest thing to deal with. I was mad at my dad for years because he rejected and abandoned me. When I would ask him why he wasn't around when I was a child, he would get nervous and change the subject or get off the phone. It was a subject he didn't want to talk about. He never answered my questions.

Around the time my dad passed away, I had a friendship that turned into a relationship. Time went passed and I noticed a lot of similarities between my new relationship and my dad. I would always hear people say you date men that are like your father. I thought that was only true if your father was present, but what if your father wasn't there for you?

His character and behavior was similar to my father. I always said I didn't want to date a man like my father and then it happened. In the beginning, he was awesome. He appeared to be everything I ever wanted and needed in a man.

As time went on, I started to see the similarities. The phone conversations began to fade away. My dad didn't like to talk on the phone. I heard the stories of how my father treated women in a negative way. He begin to treat me the same way.

Rejection and abandonment was strong in the relationship. He was there physically, but mentally and emotionally he wasn't present.

When we would get into arguments I would find myself saying you remind me so much of my dad. I don't like this. I stayed with someone that didn't make me happy because I didn't want to be alone once again.

After I would calm down he would ask me why I would say that. At first I honestly didn't know. As time went passed, I began to realize it was a familiar spirit.

A familiar spirit will connect to you without you realizing it.

When you separate from a person you might feel as if you are getting away from the rejection and abandonment. What happens when the spirit comes back into your life through another person?

Although my dad had passed away, the same spirit was in my new relationship. Everything was so familiar. The rejection spirit never left. It came in a different form, in a different person. It was a continuous cycle until I decided to destroy it once again.

I had to destroy the spirit through fasting and praying. The relationship made me feel angry, rejected, and abandoned by a man that said he loved me. *Did he really love me? Why did I feel like it was a relationship with my dad?* It wasn't a physical connection, but it was mentally and emotionally. It drained me, and I had to disconnect myself from that spirit.

CHAPTER 3

The Birthing Place

Everything starts with God.

I use to think why on earth I am her? My mother and father both abandoned me. I felt they didn't care about me. Why does existing hurt so much. Why am I here feeling so much pain?

It's hard to deal with parents not loving you correctly. I have learned over the years that some people don't know how to accept love, receive love or show love. It's a snowball effect. It's passed on from generation to generation.

Someone has to break the cycle. The person that will break the cycle will be *you*. It's very hard to change a family pattern and heal in the process. But guess what? You *can* do it and you *will* do it.

God has an amazing plan for your life. Did you know that God created you because He wants you? He thinks about you more than you think about Him. He wakes you up every morning. He allows you to see all of His beautiful creations. You can touch and smell things. You can experience life, and you can experience His love.

God created the heavens and earth. He spoke light and separated it from darkness. He created the sky, waters, stars, moon and sun. He created the fish, sea life, birds and every kind of species of flying birds, wild animals, cattle's, reptile and bugs.

Then God made us into His image and likeness. He made us godlike, reflecting His nature.

Did you know that when God created you He looked at you and was pleased with your existence?

God saw everything that He had made, and behold, it was very good (suitable, pleasant) and He *approved* it completely. Genesis 1:31 AMP

The womb of God is different from the womb of your parents. Although you may have experienced rejection from your parents, you still have everything you need.

In the beginning, God completely *approved you*. It doesn't matter how bad your parents treated you, God approved your existence. A lot of times we look at our parents as the beginning. Our parents are our original physical womb, but we are created from the womb of God. His opinion of you matters more than anything or anyone.

God *approved* humanity existence. He started with Adam. He provided Adam with the breath of life, a home, food, a job, a mate and animals. He gave Adam the authority to name each living creature. God didn't change the names Adam gave the living creature, He allowed Adam to exercise his authority. When Eve was created, all the above was waiting for her along with Adam. Everything started with Adam, but it didn't end with Adam. When God approved Adam, He approved you, too.

Let your acceptance be in God and not people, parents included.

My Father Was the First Man to Break My Heart

Growing up without a father was heart breaking for me. I saw other kids with their father; I wondered why my dad wasn't in my life. The older I got, the more it bothered me. My younger brother and I had the same mom, but different dads. He stayed with our mother and I lived with my maternal grandmother.

My brother's dad was active in his life as a child. He was around a lot; at least that's how it appeared to me. My brother's dad was always nice to me. He picked my brother up and took him places when I was a kid. I couldn't understand why my brother's dad picked him up and I knew nothing about my father. My father being absent in my life broke my heart. This was my first heart break from a man.

I didn't know much about my dad when I was a child. I only knew his first name. My grandmother didn't know much about him, either.

My parents met when they were in the army. I was born in Fort Campbell Kentucky. At seven days old my mother took me to California to live with my grandmother.

I was given my mother's last name at birth. I didn't know my dad's last name until I was 17 years old. I often wondered why he didn't look for me as child. Why didn't he try to find me? Why did he give up so easy?

As I became an adult, I found out I was conceived out of an affair. My dad was married to someone else when I was born. I guess this should have explained his absence, but I still had questions.

When I became a teenager, I told my mother that I wanted to find my dad. My mother finally told me his last name. I tried to find my dad on my own, but I couldn't. This was back in the late 90s. The internet and social media wasn't popular back then. It was at the beginning stages. I contacted a company call 1-800-us search. This company provided me every person in the USA with my dad's name.

When I got the list I was excited. But when I saw how many people in the USA had his name it was discouraging. It was at least 100 names. I was nervous and scared. I honestly didn't know what to say. It took a few moments before I would make the first call. I finally built up enough courage to start calling the list.

This is how each conversation went: *Hi my name is LiQuiche Young. I purchased a list of every person in the USA with my dad's name. I'm looking for my father. Do you have a long lost daughter? Do you know my mother?*

I gave each person my mother's name and where I was born. The last question would be, "Are you my dad"?

The person on the other end of the line would always say, "I'm so sorry sweetheart that you had to purchase a list of names and numbers to find your dad. I am not your father. I wish you the best of luck finding him."

I heard it so many times it broke my heart. The rejection turned into depression. I couldn't get through the entire list. It was too hard hearing the same answers. I can hear the hurt in each man's voice. They didn't want to break the news that they weren't my father. After call about half of the list I gave up.

My mother was mad at my grandmother and stop talking to my grandmother and me for four years. She had a life changing event and decided to start speaking to my grandmother again. I didn't like the way she handled the situation. Disappearing for four years and not speaking to me made me angry. She gave me the information on how to find my father. That was her way of saying she was sorry.

I contacted the courts and told them I was looking for my father, and asked if they could help me. They finally had good news for me. The courts told me they had my father's information. They weren't allowed to give me his information. They told me to write a letter to my dad and to send to the courts. The courts told me they would send the letter to my dad for me. I followed the courts instructions. A week later I got a call from my dad. It took me a while, but I finally found my dad. I was 17 years old.

After finding my dad and getting to know him, I found out a lot about him. I found out he kept me a secret for many years. I was an illegitimate child. In the eyes of the law my birth wasn't supposed to existence.

So that's how I felt. I always felt like I was a mistake. My life didn't matter and I had no purpose. These thoughts always came to mind in my childhood from my mother not being around, but when I found my dad I begin to feel the same emotions as an adult. It was worst because he didn't want to give me answers. The only answer I had was he cheated on his wife and I was a product of the affair and this answer wasn't from him.

My father was the first man to break my heart. Little girls want their fathers to love them, teach them how a man is supposed to treat them, show them proper affection, provide for them, teach them about men, give them flowers and be the example of a what kind of men they should date.

He missed out on so many special moments in my life. He missed out on seeing my good grades, going to school dances, award ceremonies, prom, dating, college, my first job, graduations from high school and college. He missed my first poem that was published when I was eleven years old. He wasn't around to see any of my accomplishments.

I met my dad three times in my life. He had promise to come to California to see me for over five years. He never came. I prayed about it. I asked God if I should go. My dad lived in North Carolina. I got enough courage to go.

I found out that I have a brother on my dad's side. We built a relationship. He became someone that I spoke to often. When I decided to go to North Carolina, I stayed with my brother.

It was hard getting on a plane to go see strangers that were my family. I never met my dad or brother before. It took a lot of faith to get on a plane to meet strangers and co-habitat with a stranger. I was far away from home, and alone on this journey.

When I met my dad I thought it was going to be this great reunion. My brother took me to meet him. When I met him I reached to give him a hug. I wanted to hug him tight. It was my first time seeing my dad. He gave me a pat on the back and said it's nice to see you. All I could do was laugh. In my mind I thought it was going to be like what you see on the movies.

A daughter and father see each other and they run to towards one another and embrace each other. That was truly in the movies, that didn't happen to me at all. All I could do was laugh in the inside. It was another rejection moment.

After this awkward moment, I stayed for a few hours and then I left. I think I saw him a few more times on this particular trip, and then I headed back home. I just didn't know why I put myself through this moment, but at least I made the first step to see him.

I saw him the following year. The third year I saw him was at his funeral. He passed away. He passed away and left me with so many unanswered questions. The disappointment really set in when I realized that my dad still was breaking my heart and he passed away.

At the funeral, I told myself that I wouldn't allow my dad to break my heart again. As I sat through the funeral the tears kept falling from my eyes. I was disappointed that my dad left me with so many unanswered questions. I prayed and told God I was going to close this chapter of my life. At the end of the funeral, my sister and I closed the casket on our father. As I closed the casket, I told myself I was going to leave all the hurt and pain in the casket with him. And I thought I did, but this was only the beginning of my heart being healed.

My FATHER Was The First Man To Heal My Heart.

If my father was the first man to break my heart, how can he be the first man to heal my heart? My paternal father was my earthly father. He was the father that physically birthed me into the earth. Earthly fathers mess up and make mistakes. But your heavenly FATHER makes no mistakes. It's no room for error with your heavenly FATHER.

My heavenly FATHER was the first man to heal my heart. When I first started talking to God, I had no clue what to say. I begin to talk to Him as if I was talking to a person I could see. It was hard at first, because you can't see your heavenly FATHER. You have to have faith and trust that, even though you can't see this heavenly FATHER that He is still there.

After my father's funeral, I got on a plane and came back to California. On the plane ride I thought about the funeral. I thought about my decision to let go of the hurt and pain my father caused my life. Before my father passed away, our last words to each other was I love you. Although my father didn't physically show he loved me, I actually believed him this time when he told me. I knew I had to forgive him.

As I read the Bible and other books, the healing process started to take place. I prayed that God would release my father from my heart. I didn't want to carry the hurt anymore. I knew it was time to completely forgive. Many people are upset with people that have passed away, and know it's because they haven't released the pain that's attached with that particular person.

I know it was time to release my dad so I could live my life freely. I read scriptures on forgiveness. I had to learn how to forgive my thoughts. I would say I forgive my father and at the particular moment I did. Then a week, month or year would past. I would get mad all over again when I thought of him. I had to forgive him again. I learned that forgiveness wasn't a onetime act it was a lifestyle.

I prayed to God daily. I thanked Him for teaching me how to forgive my father. In the beginning it was hard. I was angry. I had so many questions that I would never get the answers to. I understood it wouldn't happen overnight. Forgiveness was a process.

My heavenly father taught me faith. I had to have faith that one day I could forgive my father and stay in a forgiving space. My biggest challenge was forgiving my thoughts. I would sit and think about all the hurt and pain my father caused in my life. When I prayed I believed that God would take away the anger.

My heavenly father taught me patience. During this process I learned how to be patient. I wanted my actions to be pleasing in the sight of God. I wanted to rush the process of forgiving my father. Unfortunately, it doesn't work that way. It took years to break you; it will take time to completely heal you.

The Healing Process

There were two major steps that I took that aided in my healing process. These steps made it easier for me to move forward and forgive my father for abandoning me.

I had to believe that God would listen to me and heal me from rejection and abandonment. Having faith can be hard to do; especially when you've never used it to believe on a higher level. I've always believed it's no pain on earth that heaven can't heal. It would replay over and over again in my mind.

Step 1: Declare Healing

When I thought of all the agony rejection had caused me, I would make a declaration. "There is no pain that heaven can't heal. This rejection has no power over me. By His stripes I am healed. I take my authority that you my heavenly Father have given me and I receive my healing."

You must always declare the Word of God over your life and circumstances. *Look, I have given you authority over all the power of the enemy and you can walk among snakes and scorpions and crush them. Nothing will injure you.* (Luke 10:19 NLT)

Did you know the power to overcome from rejection is already given to you? You already have access to it. It's already in you to take dominion over rejection. In the book of Genesis when God created humanity, your heavenly Father gave you dominion over the earth and everything in it. (Gen 1:26 paraphrase) Rejection included.

It has no power or authority to operate in your life. You have the right to take dominion over it.

Step 2: Receive Healing

Healing is a gift from God. When Jesus died on the cross, he died for all of our sins. He died for your sins, my sins, our parents' sins and everyone else that has walked this earth. Healing comes from being in the presence of your heavenly father.

Being in the presence of your heavenly Father will restore you and make you live. (Isa 38:16) Restoring means to bring back to the former or original condition. In the Bible, you will *never* read, God created you to be rejected, abandoned and broken.

Life sometimes will throw you a curve ball. When life does this, your heavenly Father will always be there to restore you back to your original condition.

Your original condition includes power, wholeness, dominion and authority. No injuries to your soul or emotional wounds and acceptance in God.

The Umbilical Cord

The umbilical cord carries oxygen and nutrients from the placenta into the baby blood stream. The umbilical cord is connecting the baby and the mother. The cord is 3 to 4 cm from the baby belly button with a plastic clip. It makes the baby one with the mother physically.

Let's look at the biblical meaning for number three. It means the Father, Son and Holy Spirit. The biblical meaning for number four is creation.

Who are you connected to? Who carries your oxygen and nutrients? Will you choose to connect to rejection or acceptance? This is the place of rebirthing. Although you can never change who you were physically birth to, you can choose who you want to be rebirthed to.

It took me a long time to understand this. I stayed in an abusive relationship with my mother, friends and associates because of loyalty. I had plenty of opportunities to be rebirthed into a different environment, but I choose to stay.

Connecting to God qualifies me as a winner. I believe that God was there with me every step of the way. Although sometimes I didn't have people physically there to help me and walk me through the process, I had God.

The umbilical cord was the beginning stages of my rebirth and creation stages. I decided to stop communicating with my mother because I needed to be rebirthed and experience my creation stages. It was a stage of protection from pain. Making the decision to walk away from a toxic parent is never easy, but it's necessary.

If you have toxic parents you can chose to stay in the situation or take your new umbilical cord and connect it to God.

The Word of God brings healing and cleansing to your soul. The good thing about the rebirthing and umbilical cord process is you can connect back into your parents and still remain connected to God at any given time. But you must be wise. Don't disconnect out of unforgiveness, if you need to disconnect, do it to remove yourself from a toxic environment so that you can properly heal.

During your healing process, plug into God. After your healing process, stay connected to God. Once you experience acceptance from God, you won't accept anything else.

CHAPTER 4

Life without Parents

*Even if my mother and father abandon me, the
Lord will hold me close. Ps 27:10 NLT*

Imagine going through life with no parents. You are the only person on the earth. You have everything in the earth physically, but no parents. No physical person to guide you, to teach you what to do and no examples before you. You are the example.

Well this is the story of Adam and Eve. Adam and Eve were the first humans to live on earth according to the Bible. (Gen 1) They didn't have parents on earth. They didn't have a physical person to teach them, guide them or learn from them.

Adam stayed in constant communication with God in the Garden of Eden. God is all Adam knew. Adam placed His trust in God because that was his only option.

Adam was given everything he needed to survive here on earth. He was given a place to live, food to eat, a job and a mate.

God and Adam had a special meeting place in the garden. He talked to Adam daily and gave Adam instructions. Adam and Eve were the beginning of humanity. They were the first generation of people with no parents and the first generation God Fathered.

God was there for Adam and Eve and He will be there for you as well. Just like Adam and God had a meeting place, so can you and God. He is always available for you when you need Him. All you have to do is get into His presence. He wants to be your Father. He's always available for you.

He's never forceful and He's always a gentleman. He will never force you to do something against your will. You will always have free will, your own choice. It's up to you to seek God and ask Him for guidance.

The good news is you're not the first person to be parentless. God has fathered parentless people for many generations. This is nothing new for Him. He is perfectly capable of handling your situation. God has plenty of experience with dealing with fatherless and motherless people.

He understands not everyone will choose to be parents to their children. He also understands everyone will not know how to be parents. He understands sometimes He will have to take over in moments, seasons and possibly a lifetime. Parents aren't perfect; God is willing to help if the parent chooses to stay.

Just like God provided for Adam and Eve, He's waiting to supply all of your needs as well. Don't worry if your parents aren't present, God is forever present.

I remember when I first read the story about Adam and Eve. It amazed me that God was all they had. It amazed me how God created them as adults and not children. They never knew what childhood looked like. They only knew adulthood.

Reading this story inspired me so much. Every time I read it, I always remember God was with them and He is with me as. He is also with you!

Skipped Generation

When parents relinquish their duties as mom and dad, grandparents often take the role of parents. A lot of times a grandparent will become a parent to the grandchild when the parent can't financially or emotionally contribute to their child's life. This is what I like to call G.A.P: Grandparents as parents. G.A.P's usually take on this responsibility so the child doesn't have to go into foster care.

When a grandparent raises a grandchild, it can cause the parent to feel rejection. The parent will feel rejection because the grandparents are spending a lot of time with the grandchild, or the child has developed a close relationship with the grandparent. The parent can also feel rejected because the attention and focus isn't on the parent anymore; causing them to feel excluded, abandoned, envious and jealous of the child.

This is called a skipped generation. A skipped generation is when the parent is removed from the one generation and placed in a different generation. So the grandparent becomes a parent to the child. When the grandparent raises the grandchild, the grandchild becomes the child.

Biologically they're the grandparent, but the bond that is formed between the grandparent and the child has strengthened because a parent child relationship has formed.

The parent and child looks at the same person as a parent. It changes the view of the relationship because of this. In some cases, the parent and child develop a sibling type of relationship because the parent is the same person.

As a young child this is something I struggled with. My grandmother was my mother, but my mother was my mother, too. I technically had two mothers growing up.

This situation causes generational rejection. This happens because the mother rejected the child and the child rejected the mother. In this situation rejection is a learned behavior. The mother gives the child to the grandparent. The child sees the grandparent and the mother, and then the mother feels rejected because she is no longer included in the three generations, Its now two generations, which can cause emotional damage to everyone involved.

God Has Parents Waiting For You...

When a parent is absence God has people waiting to be your parent. It might not be hands over 100%, but it will be when you need a parent the most.

God has people waiting to bless you. These specific people love God and have been assigned to love you on behalf of God. When He gives instructions for your journey, He will a specific person who He trusts to fulfill the assignment that you're connected to.

So when you need help, it may not come from your birth parents, and that's okay. It may come from a stranger, a pastor, a friend, teacher, another family member etc. God will always have a way to provide you with what you need. There's always an obedient person around waiting to hear from God to bless you. You're blessing can be an encouraging word, money or someone just wanting to spend time with you. Whatever it may be, know that it will be divine and assigned.

The people that God assigned to your life will not necessary be your biological parents, but they will be parents for you when you need them. These people will come in seasons, on time, and with a divine purpose.

I remember when I truly wanted a father. God not only gave me a stepfather, but He also added two god fathers.

These men were great men in my life. I learned something from each of them. Some of them stayed in my life forever, and some was seasonal. I wasn't as close to these men as I would have liked to be, but I appreciated that God gave them to me when I needed them the most.

My childhood pastor and a few other pastors had a great impact on my life as well. They taught me about God, showed me how to experience the presence of God and created a safe place for me to grow.

Each and every person that God sent my way deposited something special in my life. They taught me life lessons, and protected me during the season God entrusted them with my life.

Remember, when you're feeling neglected or rejected by your earthly parents, seek comfort in the word of God. The Bible is full of promises, love letters and guidance to help you through life. Even when you feel alone the Bible says He is with you. He is always present. He will never leave you or forsake you, even when your parent(s) did. He will provide you with everything you need.

The love that He provides for you is unconditional. When the love your parents should have for you isn't present, know that God's love will never subside. His love is unfailing. It's impossible for His love to leave you. You are His prize possession. No matter how many people walk out your life, God's love and presence will always remain.

You may think that just because you're an adult, that you don't need the love, guidance, and wisdom from a parent, but you do. Even as an adult you still will need guidance from God. He will heal all of your emotional wounds from your childhood. Communing with God teaches you how to grow through the emotional wounds and heal those places damaged by rejection.

When you find yourself struggling with the pain of your childhood, seek God's face. You should never go a day without seeking Him. You can seek Him through prayer, reading your Bible, praise & worship, mediating on scriptures and fasting. He is always happy to hear from you.

How to Honor an Absent Parent

I remember when I was trying to find solace in my issue with my absentee parents and still honor them. I started searching for scriptures that I could relate to, and God put the story of Adam and Eve on my heart. When I first realized Adam and Eve had no parents, I was perplexed. I would read the Bible and have a hard time understanding it. I thought, *how I am supposed to relate to it? These events happened so many years ago. How am I supposed to relate this Bible story to my life currently?*

In the Bible it says God is the same yesterday, today and forever more. When I read this scripture I saw the Bible differently. That's when I realized that God is Adam and Eve's parent. I immediately knew that if God could be a parent to Adam and Eve, He could be a parent to me.

When you get a car it comes with a manual. In the manual it tells you about every function of the car. It gives details of how each part works.

I learned the Bible is the manual of God. It talks about His character, His nature, how He operates, His Spirit, how He much He loves His people He created and His instructions.

I learned how to pray, praise, worship, read the Bible and fast. This is the way to get close to God. He's always available, something that my earthly parents weren't.

I had many moments I would cry myself to sleep because I was feeling so much emotional pain from the absence of my parents. I would get on my knees and pray. The more I cried out I would feel a warm presence in my body and in my room. I knew it was God comforting me.

As a child, I was taught to respect my parents, even if they didn't honor or respect me. Honor your mother and father was a scripture I knew very well. How do you honor someone when they don't honor you, respect you or show you love?

This concept didn't make sense to me. It actually made me angry and taught me how to suppress my anger. It also made me feel very misunderstood. All they understood was you should obey your parents; you shouldn't say anything bad about them, you should honor them. But God was the only one who understood my tears.

You keep traced of all my sorrows. You have collected all my tears in your bottle. You have recorded each one in your book. Ps 56:8 NLT

I prayed to God and told Him, I just need this pain to leave my soul. I just want the burden to go away. I was tired of trying to please everyone and listen to their instructions. God I just want to tell you about this. You said in your word that you hear the prayers of the righteous.

When the righteous cry for help, the LORD hears and delivers them out of all their troubles. Ps 34:17

The more I released everyone else's standards of me, I began to feel freedom. I understood I needed to honor my parents, but no one understood that my parents had a responsibility to me as well. At that moment I knew I could honor my parents without being in relationship with them. I knew they were my parents, but I also knew it was impossible to honor someone who wasn't there.

I respected my parents, but I didn't respect the way I was treated. I loved them and forgave them for all the wrong things they did in my life. How do you meet the expectations of others definition of honor? You simply respect them.

If your parents don't respect you, it's okay to create distance between the two of you. You were *not* created to be abused or mistreated because someone gave birth to you. Treat people the way you desire to be treated, even if they don't respect you, still have respect for them.

So, how do you honor an absent parent? You honor an absent parent by being respectful. If the environment is toxic, avoid it. And always remember you *can't* force someone to do anything they don't want to do.

If your parent rejected or abandoned you, always remember that it was their personal choice. Not yours. You must continue to live life. Wake up every day with purpose and passion, Regardless of how others feel about you.

Accepted By God

CHAPTER 5

Acceptance from God

For you created my inmost being; you knit me together in my mother's womb. Ps 139:13 NIV

*I*f God loves me why did He allow these things to happen to me? Why do I feel emotionally abused and why do I feel emotionally suppressed? How in the world can God truly accept me? Where is the love at?

These questions played in my mind over and over again; and no one could answer my questions so I stopped asking them. But deep down inside I still had these questions. I prayed to God and didn't understand why I wasn't getting an answer. I was upset with God because I felt like His protection wasn't there.

I felt isolated and alone for many, many years. I went to church, read my Bible and did my best to live my life according to the Bible and loved others. I didn't understand why I didn't receive the love I gave to others that rejected me.

The love always came in different places and not the places I wanted or thought I needed love from. I learned the hard way that you can't force people to love you.

At times I felt like God was rejecting me as well. I was hurt and confused. My main question was "God why me"? Why am I experiencing so much pain in my soul?

As time went on, I learned that God wasn't the reason why my parents rejected and abandoned me. God gives us all free choice and free will.

In our free choices comes with both rewards and consequences. Unfortunately my life was a product of the consequences of my parents' free will. I felt like my life was mishandled because of the decisions my parents made.

Since my mother gave me to my grandmother to raise me, and my father was absent from my childhood and most of my adult life, during my entire childhood I thought I was a mistake.

I thought God over looked my situation and nothing good could be birthed from the pain I was experiencing. I was angry as a child and angry as an adult.

Since my anger was suppressed, I didn't learn how to release it properly. Whenever I did release anger, it was yelling and expressing my frustration. It was throwing things, hitting the wall, screaming loud and speaking hurtful words.

The anger I had inside of me was immature. I didn't know how to verbally express myself, because I thought it would make me disrespect my elders. Instead of talking about how I was feeling, I suppressed my true emotions. I thought I was doing some good, but suppressing my anger intensified it even more.

When I became an adult my anger wasn't respectful. It was if I would vomit words to anyone who would listen. I was angry! When I looked at myself, I saw a painful angry woman. I saw myself trapped in my emotions. I knew I had to view my life differently. I learned that faith would get me through the rejection process and guide me to acceptance. I was desperate to experience God's love and compassion. Faith was the vehicle to get me there.

Learning acceptance from God is learning to be loved by God. The love of God is unconditional, it's everlasting and it's always available for you. He accepts *you*!

You don't have to worry about suppressing your feelings in your relationship with God. You can express yourself to God freely in prayer. You can cry your eyes out to God. He will listen, He will comfort you, and He will help you and lead you out of anger to and into love.

Embracing Acceptance

For so many years I felt rejected by my parents. That rejection carried over into my relationships with other family members, my work environment, friendships and relationships. I lived in a bubble of rejection. *How do I pop this bubble?* I thought to myself. I realized that I was struggling with acceptance, and needed to embrace being accepted by those who cared about me.

I didn't grasp how important embracing acceptance was at the time. Acceptance actually leads you down the road of healing. The acceptance journey took a lot of prayer, patience with myself, self-evaluation, journal writing and seeing a therapist.

I was taught "any failure in life is a prayer failure". I had to ask God to teach me how to accept myself. I was comfortable with not feeling important and abandoned. *How do I change that?*

All my changes came through my relationship with God. I learned that God *did* love me, even in those moments when I felt like He wasn't present or near me.

I learned in those moments God was teaching me to have faith. I had to learn to believe that God would never leave me or forsake me, just like His word says. I had to also learn how to keep the faith in my darkest moments in life.

Learning how to embrace acceptance gets worse before it gets better. Life's biggest lesson in this process is to learn, unlearn and relearn again. How does this work? Let me explain the process.

My mother taught me what rejection and abandonment looked like and how it felt. This was learning behavior from my environment. This was something I saw with my own eyes, it was my life experiences. I was very good at accepting the learned behaviors of rejection.

When you get in the presence of God, these feelings are still there in the beginning. I learned that God doesn't want you to completely forget the experience, but He wants you be healed from it. He wants to heal your thoughts, emotions and soul. Once you're healed from your own wounds, then you can help someone else.

When it comes to unlearning these behaviors, this is when you'll need to separate from the environment these behaviors were learned. You can't heal in the place you received the hurt. After I understood this, that was conformation for me that separation from my mother was a *must*.

Once you separate from your parents, you can't allow guilt and condemnation to stop the process. The separation is necessary. You also must be patience with the process. It took years to learn the behaviors and it's possible it will take years to unlearn them.

During this process you must stay prayerful and ask God for guidance. In the unlearning process, you will be taught how to detox from rejection and abandonment. It's a shift of the mind. All the negative thoughts and feelings you experienced in the place of rejection, will be transformed. This is the space where you will make a conscious effort to renew your mind.

You must renew your mind with the word of God. Read at least one scripture a day and meditate on it. It's okay to mediate on the same scripture everyday if you feel it's necessary. If you don't know where to start at, I recommend you start in the book of Psalms. It has a lot of healing and uplifting scriptures to read.

The relearning process teaches you to receive acceptance and love. This is your new environment. During this process, you will experience isolation and separation. Any remaining fruit of rejection will be destroyed from the root.

The relearning process is confusing. If you're not careful, you can misinterpret this stage as rejection.

I had to learn how to love God and myself. Throughout this phase, I wanted to go back to the land of familiar. Why would I want to go back to the land of familiar? My familiar place was rejection. I wanted to go back to the people that hurt me. Not because I enjoyed being hurt but because that is what I knew.

Every time I felt this way I had to remember the steps that were required to get to acceptance and love. I had to be willing to relearn and not go back to the learning stage.

The stage of learning is what taught me rejection. I had to learn how to trust the process of acceptance. The process of acceptance was the place of unfamiliar territory.

The place of unfamiliar territory is the place God teaches you how to love Him, yourself and others. This is where God needs to protect you the most. This is why isolation is necessary. Your surroundings will change. People will come and go. You will learn how to protect yourself and your new environment.

This is also the stage God will heal you from the places and people who destroyed you. Once you have accepted your new life, God will put you on public display. He will prepare a table before you in the presence of your enemy.

I just want to make it very clear that your parents are not your enemy. Anything that goes against the will of God is an enemy. The public display will show everyone that your cup is running over. It's your place of love, healing and restoration.

People once viewed you as broken, but now they see you as healed and restored. When you are restored, you are the original version of who God created you to be before the rejection took place.

Once you have experienced all three of these stages, you can evaluate if you're strong enough to try and rebuild a relationship with your parents. If your parents are sorry for the way they treated you, it makes it easy to work towards restoring the relationship.

If your parents aren't sorry or doesn't show remorse, then it's your decision if you want to be in an environment full of rejection again.

If you decide to go back to the relationship, you will repeat steps 1 through 3 all over again. It's very important to protect yourself and not engage in relationships that aren't healthy for you.

When trying to restore a relationship both or all parties must be willing to restore. Forgiveness must take place on both ends. This is the only way the relationship can be restored.

Pray to God and ask Him when you should seek restoration.

You Deserve Acceptance

When you've been rejected for so long, knowing that you deserve acceptance can be challenging. Acceptance is when people love you just the way you are. Other people's opinion of your life isn't pushed or forced upon you. Even in your wrong doings, others will love you while you're trying to figure life out.

A parent's job is to lead, guide, protect and nurture you to the best of their ability. A part of their role as your parent is to accept you the way that you are. This was not what I experienced with my mom.

Although my family thought it was biblically right to create a relationship between my mother and I, it wasn't the best choice for me. They wanted us to have a loving and affectionate relationship, but it's not something that we shared.

As I got older I made my own choices for myself. I decided to end the relationship between my mother and I. The relationship was extremely toxic, I felt heavy and I had no peace. I decided I wasn't going to allow someone to be abusive emotional and physical to me because they gave me life.

Just because a person is your parent doesn't mean you have to take abuse, verbal or physical, from them. The moment I decided to terminate the relationship I immediately felt free. The Bible says to guard your heart; Out of it are the issues of life.

My mother was definitely an issue that I had, so it was best to guard myself from her.

When I became an adult it was my job to protect me. Not the way others thought I should be protected, but the way I knew I should be protecting myself.

When I learned that my life and feelings mattered just like my parents did, I learned to focus on the things that made me happy. I focused on my relationship with God, passion and purpose. I figured out why I'm on this earth.

I didn't go through rejection and abandonment for nothing. It was for a reason and a purpose. I learned to accept the woman I had become, flawed childhood and all.

Do I like the fact that I had to carry this pain throughout life? Absolutely not! But I've learned that I had to go through a test to get to the testimony.

The Bible says that we are overcome by the power of our testimony. I'm thankful that I have the opportunity to share my test and my testimony. If God can heal me from the pain and terror of my childhood, He can do the same for you.

You deserve acceptance, love and peace. No one should feel depressed, anxiety or emotional torment because a particular person in their lives, especially not from the person that is supposed to protect you. This is how I felt when I was connected to my mother. I didn't have choice as a child, but as an adult I had options.

The moment I realize I had options and didn't have to deal with my mother, my healing began to take place. I started to feel like I deserved to be loved.

Being accepted is being love. God is love so when you experience Him, love is what you feel. The love the world provided is different from what God provides. That's the love you want to accept. And know that's the love that you deserve.

You're One of a Kind

One question that will come to your mind at some point and time is "Who Am I". It's so many ways to answer that question. Some people will identify themselves with their job, house, cars, accomplishments, family etc. I'm referring to who you are at the core of your essence. Who are you in the sight of God?

Have you ever thought about how special God created you? You're unique and your creation is handmade. Let's explore the uniqueness God made you.

You Were Born At a Unique Set Time in History. The year you were born is special. God was mindful about the specific time and season that He released you into the earth. He could have created you during the 1500s, 1600s, 1700s etc. He chooses the year; He chooses for specific reason. You were born at the right time, with the right people and in the right place. The year you were born was *not* a mistake.

The Place You Were Born. God was mindful of the place you were born. I was born in an army hospital in Kentucky. My mother's side of the family is from California. At 7 days old I came to California to live with my grandmother. It wasn't a mistake that I was born in a different state away from family. God has a way of creating you're your life story from being to the end. We may not understand but He does. Your birth place was *not* a mistake.

What Time Were You Born? The time you were born was the time God wanted you to make your grand entrance into the world.

Your Birthday!! This is your special day. Celebrate your existence even if others don't. This is the day purpose was birthed in the earth. Your birthday matters.

The Family You Were Birthed Into

You might wonder if God birthed you into the wrong family because of rejection. It's very easy to feel that way when your parents rejected you. God makes no mistakes. You were birthed in the right family.

The genetic makeup of your family is what God needed to create you. If you didn't stay with your biological family after birth it's okay. You were still birth into the right family. Blood doesn't make you family. Blood makes you related. Love makes you family.

The Genetic Makeup of You

God was mindful of your genetic makeup when He created you. The color of your eyes, your facial features, your skin color and skin tone, your hair color, your height. Birth marks are his love marks. Your physical appearance is God's beauty.

> *And the very hairs on your head are all numbered (Matt 10:30 NLT)*

It's great that God knows how many hairs you have on your head. But it's amazing that your hairs on your head are numbered. It's a difference between knowing how many hairs you have on your heads and knowing the number. God can look at the center of your head and identify what number the hair is.

Can you image God saying this is hair number 10, this is hair number 20, this is hair number 30 oh and this is hair number 100? He's positive of those numbers because He places them there.

Your Name Has Special Meaning

Have you ever looked up your name? Do you know what your name means? I did a lot on research on my name. LiQuiche (pronounced Lakesha) I couldn't find anything on the spelling of my name. My name is spelled very unique. So when I did research I searched for Lakesha. This is what I found.

Arabic Origin: Alive and well

African origin: Favorite

Hebrew origin: Cassa Tree

Irish origin: Favorite

English Origin: Great Joy and happy

Swahili Origin: Favorite one

My name means Her Life.

Every time I felt down I had to remember what my name means. I had to look myself in the mirror and call out my own name. I am Alive and well, I am the favorite one, I am great joy, I am happy and the favorite.

My name is a great reminder that my life matters. I am a great joy to be around and I'm God's favorite in my eyes, although God doesn't love any of His children more than another.

When someone calls your name, what are they saying about you? What does your first name mean? *(Take the time to research your name)*.

If you find something bad associated with your name ignore it. That's not the right meaning for you. My middle name is Lee.

Old English Meaning: pasture or meadow

Latin Meaning: Lion

American Meaning: Healer

Dictionary definitions the sheltered side; the side away from the wind. And Sheltered from the wind.

Once I understood my middle name, it was the second conformation of my purpose. I always knew I had a purpose. No matter how I felt I knew I belonged here on earth, even when my parents rejected and abandoned me.

When I look in the mirror, I see a place of shelter looking back on me when I don't feel emotionally safe. I am protected when I feel unsafe. I am safe because my name means safety. When someone calls your name, what are they saying about you?

My last name is Young.

Dictionary definition: Being in the first, or early stage of life or growth; youthful, not old.

It means a separation from generation and the younger one. When someone calls your name, what are they saying about you?

I would like to encourage you to look up the meaning of your name. If you can't find the meaning of your name the way its spelled looks it up in a different spelling. If you find something bad associated with your name ignore it. That's not the right meaning for you.

I'm sure when my mother named me she had no clue what these names mean, but this is the name God wanted me to have. When people call your name who are they really calling? It more than just names, when people call your name what are they really saying about you?

CHAPTER 6

Got Faith?

What is faith? It is the confident assurance that something we want is going to happen. It is the certainty that what we hope for is waiting for us, even though we cannot see it up ahead.
Hebrews 11:1 (TLB)

From rejection to acceptance is a journey. Although the journey is difficult it is possible. With faith, determination, and a strong desire to heal, you can definitely make it happen.

Faith is having full confidence in God that He will provide you restoration. In the process it may look like it's very little light at the end of the tunnel. Having faith is simply trusting God through the process, with no physical evidence.

Trusting God through the process will strengthen your faith. You will overcome mountains, be strengthened in your valleys and learn how to trust God as your coming out of rejection.

Your faith will provide you with big and small victories. Faith help you get through the pain when it seems impossible. Faith is your tour guide through your darkest moments in life.

Having Faith Daily

Some people may think that having faith is hard. We use faith daily and don't realize it. God has given each of us a measure of faith. When you wake in the morning to get up, do you wonder will your legs work? Nope, you just get up and walk.

When get in your car to go to work, do you wonder if your car will start? Of course not! Because you trust that your car is working perfectly fine.

When you sit in a chair do you wonder if the chair can hold you up? Do you wonder if it will break, or do you just sit in the chair?

If you are adventurous and get on rides at an amusement park, do you wonder will the ride stop working? Do you wonder if the ride will stop while you're hanging upside down and leave you stuck there for hours? You sure do not! You will get on multiple rides and enjoy your visit at the Amusement Park.

Those types of thoughts never enter your mind. It never enters your mind because God already gave you a measure of faith. Since you see you already have a measure of faith, now it's time to learn how to grow your faith.

Faith + Healing + Restoration = Deliverance

Now that we understand faith, let's talk about the benefits of faith. Faith is simply belief. You believe that life will get better. No matter what your current circumstances are, you must believe that God will restore all areas of your life, with no physical evidence.

You must believe the pain of rejection will go away some day. Rejection is something that you experience inside and outside of family. The rejection from your parents is just the beginning. The world is waiting to provide you with more rejection. It's waiting for you no matter what. You must learn to embrace and overcome it.

When you feel rejected, it's an opportunity for God to show you how much He loves you. When you become angry and feel emotional turmoil, ask yourself why you feel that way. Your faith will teach you how to redirect the rejection.

The Bible says to cast all your cares onto Him because He cares for you. You weren't designed to carry rejection. It's your responsibility to give it back to God immediately.

If your parents rejected you as a child, don't worry that you carried it. You weren't old enough to know what rejection was and how to give it to God through faith. The good news is now you have the ability to give it to God now.

Rejection comes in seasons, but you will definitely experience it throughout life. Seasons of rejection looks confusing. During these specific seasons it becomes intense, draining and overwhelming physically, mentally and emotionally. When you experience rejection on this level, you will learn how to fight for your restoration.

Seasonal rejection will come to test your faith. It comes to teach you how to maintain your restoration. Not to say that when God heals you one time it isn't enough. During each season of restoration, you will learn a different side of God you didn't know before.

In one season He could be an emotional healer, a mind regulator, shelter from enemies, teaching you how to use words of affirmations etc.

So when the attack comes don't think God didn't restore you, He's teaching you how to maintain your restoration. This is the beginning stages of your deliverance.

Your Faith Gives You Deliverance

You must use your faith to receive deliverance. Receiving deliverance is simply being set free. God wants to set you free from rejection. The question is: will you allow Him to do it? Will you trust His process? When you experience rejection, you must keep your restoration that God gave you. You have to learn how to stay free.

CHAPTER 7

Pray For Parents That Rejected You!

Steps on getting to the place where you can pray for the person that rejected you!!!

This is a subject that a lot of people won't understand. How in the world am I supposed to pray for someone that rejected me? Especially my parents. The person that was supposed to love me and care for me. You don't understand how much that hurt me! How is that humanly possible for me to pray for them?

Well, the Bible says in Luke 6:28 NIV *"Bless those who curse you, pray for those who mistreat you."*

This is not an easy task, but it can be done. When someone hurts you, the first thing you want to do is hurt them back. The pain that they caused, you just want it to go away. Sometimes you might even want that person to feel how you feel. Do you know how to let go of the pain? You overcome it. Here are four ways to overcome your pain:

1. **The first step is to acknowledge the pain.**

   Rejection is a painful event, and it's real. If you block it out as if it never happened to you, you're only suppressing the memories. It will come and go. It will haunt you. It will come up in your dreams, it will become a nightmare. A mental recorder will constantly repeat in your head. The event will never go away until you acknowledge it happened.

I remember the first time I had to address the pain of rejection I was feeling. The pain was double for me because I felt rejection from both parents. The effects of the pain started to overpower my life. I had no idea what it was, but it was real. It effected how I showed up in the world. I was shy as a child and I hated being the center of attention.

By Acknowledging the pain you are no longer a victim but you're victorious.

2. **The second step is to make a decision that rejection is no longer your home.**

   Your home is your resting place; a place that you have peace. It's the dwelling where you can relax, where you can have comfort, shut out the negative things and connect with your inner peace.

   I decided I no longer want to be in a hurting place, in a dark place, in a place where rejection was a lifestyle. I said enough is enough. You have to make a decision that you will not live a rejected lifestyle.

3. **The third step is taking back control over your life.**

You have full control of who you want to have in your life. If someone is disturbing your peace, you have the choice not to associate with that person. You only get one life, make it a happy one.

Although you were rejected growing up, you don't have to stay in a state of mental rejection. The memories will be there, but you can overcome the pain of your past. It's time to take control.

4. **The fourth step is to accept it happened to you.**

This is one of the hardest things to do. At some point you will ask yourself why this was your experience. Sometimes bad things happen to good people. Sometimes people don't know how to treat others. Sometimes parents don't know how to be parents. Sometimes parents don't want to be parents. Sometimes God allows things to happen and we don't understand why. Sometimes you're strong enough to stand in the storm without being swept away.

Whatever the case may be, it happened and it happened to you. That doesn't mean that you are not loved. So many people in the world love you. Focus on love and not the rejection.

Now that you have accepted the fact it's happened to you, you can reach out to help others.

5. **The fifth step is to release unforgiveness.**

Unforgiveness is a disease to the soul, body and mind. It constantly eats at you. It causes you to feel uneasy and brings up bad memories. It triggers negative thoughts and replays bad events in your mind.

Did you know unforgiveness causes someone to live in your head, mind and heart?

Did you know when you constantly think about the things your parents has done to you, you are holding them hostage?

Did you realize your parents are not even aware of how much you are thinking about the past?

Years and decades could pass you by, they are living their lives, not even thinking about the things that they did or didn't do for you. Release them and forgive.

CHAPTER 8

Why Should I forgive?

Forgiveness is not for others;
Forgiveness is for YOU!

I remember when I started my forgiveness journey with my parents. I had to learn how to forgive them individually and as a unit.

I had two major people in my life that rejected me and I needed to learn how to forgive them. My parents were my biggest blessing. They taught me so much without being physically there.

It took me a long time to understand it. I thought it was a curse that they rejected me. I eventually realized that I needed to forgive and release them. I've learned that your outlook and the way you perceive situations and circumstances is what matters the most.

When you don't forgive someone you hold them hostage in your heart. They're hostage in your heart and they're not aware you have them there. You carry the hurt for years and decades and you don't even realize it.

One day I asked myself "Why am I so angry?" Why do I feel like I have the right to get mad and stay mad at people? Why am I constantly getting hurt? Why can't I hurt my parents the way they hurt me? Why do I want to get revenge on people when they hurt me?"

I began to see a therapist because I knew I had an issue. I knew I had an issue when I broke up with a boyfriend in my past. The break up felt like the end of the world. It felt as if my heart and soul was ripped out of my chest in a thousand pieces and no one could glue them back together.

When I went to see my therapist she asked me why was I there. I told her I have a heart break. And then I asked, how long a heart break takes to heal. She told me it normally takes about six weeks to recover from a heart break.

She began to ask me questions about my relationship. She asked questions like, "Why did ya'll break up? Why are you taking it so hard?"

I began to answer the questions. The questions started getting more intense as she asked me questions about my childhood. She asked me what my relationship was like with my father. I told her I didn't know my father very well. I found my father when I was 17 and I didn't meet him until I was 27. He died a few years later.

She then asked me questions about my mother. Did I know my mother? How was it growing up with her? I told her my mother was in and out my life. My mother spent more time being mad at me and not talking to me more than having a relationship with me. The more I discussed my parents I began to cry.

At that moment I knew I had some soul searching. I was angry and I needed to forgive. In order to forgive I knew I needed to talk about it. And talking about it was hard.

When I would talk about it to family and friends, it would come out as anger and rage because no one understood me. Honestly, I barely understood my own emotions.

As I lay on the couch all the reasons why I shouldn't forgive my parents popped into my head. I began to cry. It was the first time in 25 years I felt like someone actually heard me, someone actually understood; I had someone that didn't judge me, someone who actually cared about how I felt. I felt like someone listened to understand me and not listened to respond.

I was so excited that I finally had someone to just listen. I didn't want anyone to take sides, but I just needed an ear to hear and not look at the situation one sided.

I continued to go the therapist because it was helping me. I had peace that I could say how I felt without anyone just carelessly quoting the Bible. I actually had someone who tried to help me through my emotions using practical advice. While I appreciate the prayers and words of comfort from scripture, at the time I needed something a little more hands-on.

I truly believe that God provides His children with a balance, which is why He gave certain people the gift of healing others through therapy.

I continued going to see the therapist. It was working. It truly helped to me talk to someone who wasn't emotionally invested into my life. The therapist told me she wanted to get to the root of the problem and she did.

While I continued receiving help with getting to the root of my anger, I also strengthened my spiritual life. I got back into church. I started praying more, reading my Bible and listening to worship music.

After the break up with my boyfriend I stayed single for five years. I didn't date anyone. I needed to heal. I had 25 years of hurt that I needed to get rid of. I knew it wouldn't be an overnight process.

The therapist told me to get a journal and write out my thoughts and feelings. I put it in a place no one could find it. I wrote in my journal daily. Some days it was good and other days it wasn't. I began to write out every memory I had in my life. The more I wrote the more I experienced mixed emotions.

Some emotions were happy, sad, rejection, abandonment, anger and rage. After I would write, I would began to ask myself questions. *Why did that thought make me feel this way? Why am I so angry?*

Every time I would write I would always hear in my mind, "We need to get to the root of this." The more I wrote, the more my life made sense.

A lot of things I experienced in my life made me mad and upset with my parents. Most of my anger was with my mother. My dad wasn't around much, so I didn't have a lot of anger towards him; it was more towards my mom.

I began to read books about anger, emotions and forgiveness. I would do research online and go to the library. I needed to understand this negative emotion I felt often. I needed to know how to get rid of it.

I then realized the source of my anger was rejection and abandonment. My therapist told me this before in one of my sessions. I didn't understand what she meant when she told me I was dealing with rejection and abandonment issues.

When other people would tell me that it would make me upset. I didn't understand why it made me upset I just knew it did. This is when I started my forgiveness process and journey.

I would read my Bible every day. The Bible became my favorite book to read. Some things I didn't understand, so I read the Bible in different translations. I would read scriptures about forgiveness, love, joy and peace. I would read them every day, I would look up the definition.

I dedicated my life to being healed emotionally from this hidden disease. I call it a disease because a disease is anything that hurts; harms or stops your body from working the way God designed it to work. It's a dis-easing feeling.

The scripture I had the hardest with was forgiving others so God can forgive you. (Mat 6:4NLT) I always thought, *but God you don't know how this made me feel, you don't understand how bad this hurts, why do I need to forgive them, they don't deserve forgiveness God.*

I thought forgiveness was unfair. It took me a long time to understand forgiveness was a gift from God. Forgiveness is a choice, forgiveness is freedom, and forgiveness is for me.

You can choose to hold the person hostage in your heart or you could choose to let it go. I thought about forgiving my parents for years before I actually did it. I didn't know how to forgive them, but I knew I needed to. I knew I had to so I could have a better life because I was bitter.

I continued to go to church, read my Bible and see the therapist. As I continued to listen to the messages preached by a pastor, it seemed like the pastor was talking directly to me, although the church was filled with hundreds of other people. God knows exactly what we need. If you ask Him for help He will help you. The help comes in ways we don't expect it to.

One day the pastor did an altar call at the church. He said, *if you have an offense against your parent or parents come to the altar now. God wants to heal you and take away the emotional pain.* I knew I was supposed to respond, so I did.

The pastor prayed and I immediately felt the presence of God. I began to feel peace in my mind, heart and soul. The more the pastor prayed, the more I felt all the hurtful emotions leaving my soul. I felt refreshed and renewed.

Deliverance was taking place and I wasn't aware of it. It was the beginning of my forgiveness journey. My pastor said you gave this hurt to God; don't take it back from Him.

When I went home I felt like a new person. I was happy because I finally felt like I forgave my parents for rejecting and abandoning me. At this point in my life I didn't see my mother at all. It was always seasons when she wouldn't talk to me.

I hadn't seen my mother in a few years. I saw her shortly after I made the decision to forgive her. When I saw her, I immediately got mad again. I was upset, angry and I felt rage. I had to walk away from her. I made an appointment to see my therapist again. I told the therapist about my wonderful experience at church. I also told her about the anger I felt when I saw my mother again.

The therapist allowed me to talk. She asked me why was I so mad when I saw my mother when I forgave her. It was a question I couldn't answer. It felt good to talk about what happened, but I also wanted to know how can I forgive and keep forgiving. I then realized forgiveness wasn't a onetime event, it was a life style.

The more I prayed and read my Bible I realized when you forgive you must continue to forgive. I had to learn how to forgive the act that happened and the thoughts when they come. This is what I mean by you can't hold people hostage in your heart.

The deep pain and rejection I experienced from my parents, I was the only one who can express how it felt. I was the only one who knows how much it damaged my life. I was the only one that has the power to forgive my parents and the thought of what they did or didn't do.

Mastering Emotions through Forgiveness

As time went on, I mastered how to forgive the acts of the past. Now I had to learn how to forgive my thoughts, my memory and anything that reminded me of the past.

Forgiveness is a process and a journey. It's something you must work at every day. It's something you must partner with God to accomplish. It is a stronghold only God can break.

When I decided to forgive my mother, I thought it was the end of my journey, but it was only the beginning. I knew that I would see her again eventually. When I saw her I didn't want to feel anger and rage. I prepared myself for that moment.

I continued to do the things that was working for me, but I had to take it a step further; I had to learn how to controls my thoughts.

I would have good days and I would have bad days. I learned that disappointments would always take me back to the moments of feeling rejected and lead me to depression. I learned not to expect anything from people, but become grateful about everything.

When I was a child my mother would buy me gifts. When she would get mad at me she would take her gift back. I remember I use to cry a lot as a child when my mother did this to me. My grandmother told my mother she wasn't allowed to buy me gifts anymore. She didn't like how I would cry when my mother would give me things and then take it away when she was mad.

As an adult it was very hard for me to accept gifts from people. It made me uncomfortable to accept gifts. My biggest fear was I would enjoy the gifts and when that person was mad at me they would take it. That was my mindset for many years as an adult.

I had to learn that every person wasn't like my mother. I had to learn it wasn't normal to receive gifts and the person takes it back when they're upset with me. That was a memory that was connected to my childhood. It was an automatic way of thinking for me.

When I made a decision to forgive the past, it began to replay in my mind over and over and over again. The thoughts would replay in my mind like a T.V show.

I found myself day dreaming about the things that happened in my childhood. I would get mad at the thought of it. I would begin to speak about it and get angry for no reason.

Rejection had begun to control my thoughts. I made up in my mind and heart that I would forgive. I would no longer hold anyone a prisoner in my heart. The moment I cleared my heart, then it entered my head and got back into my heart.

I noticed it was a cycle and I needed to end it. I continued to write in my journal, pray, read my Bible, go to church and see a therapist. In the beginning I needed to see the therapist a lot. It was a big help. I eventually got to a point where I saw the therapist less. The therapist wasn't available 24/7 but God was. I could get on my knees and pray at 3am in the morning. God was available to hear me. *He never slumbers nor sleeps.* Psalm 121:4bNIV.

> *I learned that Gods eyes are never closed. The eyes of the LORD are everywhere, keeping watch on the wicked and the good.* (Proverbs 15:3 NIV).

The more I read these scriptures I started to believe it. I kept declaring the Word day and night. One of my favorite scriptures is Josh 1:8NLT. *Study this book of Instruction continually. Mediate on it day and night so you will be sure to obey everything written in it. Only then will you prosper and succeed in all you do.*

I learned to mediate on the Word and not the past. Only then will I prosper and succeed in all I do. The more I studied this I realized that forgiving others, my thoughts and myself began with me.

I read 2 Corinthians 10:5b I read it as: *"I (LiQuiche Young) will take every captive thought and make it obedient to Christ.* It was something about inserting my name and making it personal. You have to personalize the scripture. The Bible is written for you to improve your life and learn the ways of God.

In the beginning (before all time) was the Word (Christ) and the Word was with God, and the Word was God Himself. John 1:1 AMP

The Word of God and Christ are one. I had to learn how to make my thoughts one with God through reading the Bible. The Bible saved my life.

You Must Forgive Yourself

So now there is no condemnation for those who belong to Christ Jesus (Romans 8:1 NLT).

Situations and circumstances can cause you to hold on to offenses and not forgive others or yourself. When you let old memories constantly replay in your mind it causes damage. When you ponder on the past, it allows your past to become your future. In the process of forgiving others you must learn how to forgive yourself.

In the process of my forgiving my parents I had to learn how to forgive myself. I had to forgive myself for being so hard on myself, allowing the situations and circumstances to affect me, engaging into anger, rage, and disappointment in myself and self-rejection.

Self-rejection grows like a planted tree. Self-rejection plants seeds of doubt and unbelief in your mind. I started to believe I wasn't good enough to do things in life; I rejected myself before others had the chance to reject me. I was quiet, shy, fearful and timid. I was the opposite of what God said I was. I had to renew my mind with the word of God.

For God has not given us a spirit of fear and timidity, but of power, love, and self-discipline. 2 Timothy 1:7NLT

I had to learn how to grow in forgiveness with myself. Forgiving me was a hard thing to do. I had to allow myself to grow; most importantly I had to allow myself to make mistakes. I hated making mistakes, especially if I thought it would deeply hurt someone else.

As I went through the process of forgiving me I learned more about myself. God showed me things about myself that I didn't like. I had to learn how to give myself grace, just like God gave me grace. I had to learn how to forgive me, the same way God forgave me. I learned how to renew my mind with the Word of God.

I read a story in the Bible about Paul and Silas. Paul and Silas went to jail for preaching the gospel. In the jail, they prayed and sang praises to God. While they prayed and praised God, the other prisoners *heard* them. And suddenly it was a great earthquake and shaken the foundations of the prison. Sincere prayer and praise will get the attention of God and others.

I love this story because it gives you clear instructions on what to do when you are in prison. To be in prison is not always a physical prison. A prison is a place of confinement; it's a hold place and a place to await a sentencing.

Worship got me through hard times in life, but so did my praise. My place of imprisonment was rejection. When I gave God my pure praise and true worship, the walls of rejection can tumbling down.

Rejection will cause you to become a prisoner in your heart. The heart becomes a holding place where you hold others hostage, but you also hold yourself hostage as well. When you don't forgive yourself you become a prisoner to rejection.

Rejection is trapped inside of you. The foundation is strong. You must breakthrough and break out of rejection with praise and prayer. When Paul and Silas prayed and praise God an earthquake shocked the jail and immediately all doors were open and everyone's bands were loosed.

The same thing still happens today. Prayer and praise shakes up a foundation. The more you pray and praise God, its storing up an earthquake to shake up your spirit. An earthquake is a violent shaking of the ground and the foundation. It causes a great destruction. The destruction creates damage so something no longer exists or cannot be repaired.

When you pray and give God praise, He is destroying the rejection into a thousand pieces. He is breaking it up so it can no longer come together as one. He is taking it all away from you.

The residual of rejection won't be found. The pieces will leave your body. No evidence will be found. Your prayer and praise destroys the foundation of rejection. Praise and worship is the strategy to your break through and break out.

God didn't create you to carry the worries of the world. He created you give the cares of the world to Him. It was never yours to keep. He didn't design you for stress or torture. God knew rejection would come. That's why He gave you the options to take your burdens to Him and leave them there.

Allow God to start and finish the process of healing you from rejection. Get in the presence God and do everything you can to receive healing.

Rejection from the womb was your beginning, but now you know you're accepted by God. Always remember God's love for you is unfailing. No matter how many mistakes you make, God loves you and you're accepted by God!

Final Thoughts...

Rejected from the Womb, Accepted by God is my life. God gave me this title in 2007. I was hurt and wounded from life and everything it had given me.

My mother was in and out of my life through my childhood. I didn't find my dad until I was 17 years old. I live in California and my dad lived in North Carolina. My mother gave me to her mother when I was 7 days old.

I have siblings, but none of us were raised together. My mother has two kids. We were raised in separate households. My dad has 4 kids. I didn't meet them until I became an adult.

I felt rejected and abandoned by my parents. I often asked myself why on earth I am here. Why did I have to grow up different? Why did I feel so alone when I had a lot of family around?

I was hurt, broken and lost with no identity. I had no clue who I was. All I knew was I felt pain and torture in my soul. It was a pain I couldn't explain. My life made absolutely no sense. My life looked nothing like my cousins or friends at school. Why was my life so different? What did I do so wrong?

My grandmother was my support system. I have no complaints about her. She was a strong woman of God, great courage, tremendous strength and full of faith.

But there was always something missing.

I often asked myself why I wasn't with my parents like other children were. It was a void in my life. No matter what I did it just always seem like it could never be filled. I would exercise, hang out with friends, get in to relationships, school, working, dancing, listening to music and occupying myself with family. None of that seem to work.

I still felt an empty void deep down inside of me that I couldn't seem to fill. It wasn't until I came to a certain point that I realized that I was feeling rejection. It started when I was a child. The seed was planted and it blossomed into a tall tree.

I often sat and reflected and I notice patterns in my life. Past experiences that I remember so vividly became clear. It was as if the pain of rejection and abandonment never went away.

I was raised in a Christian church. Once I turned 18, I left the church. I figured, life doesn't make sense anyway why continue to go? If God was real why did He allow me to suffer so much?

Why did I watch other children have parents and not appreciate them? Why did my father abandon me? Why did my father pass away and leave me here on earth with so many unanswered questions? WHY, WHY, WHY???

I searched for this answer for many years and I eventually found out why.

When I was 24 years old, I was at the worst state of my life. Three important people in my life passed away in four months. I was devastated. I had no clue on how to handle it. The walls of pain closed in on me. I felt heavy. I was always sad. I cried until I couldn't cry anymore.

At that time, I was out of church for at least six years. I told myself when I found a church door that was open I would go in there and see if God would talk to me, if He would just listen to me. *Lord I just need to get this hurt and pain off my chest.*

Not only did I deal with rejection, abandonment, pain and torture, something new was added on. It was always there, but the presence was strong. It's called grief and separation.

Would God really take the burden away? I was taught He would if I would only give it to Him. Would He really carry this burden that has made my life so heavy like the Bible says?

I walked into a local church in my area. As I sat in the seat, I couldn't listen to what the preacher had to say. I was looking for God's presence. I saw God work in the adult's lives in church growing up. Now it was my time for Him to work in my life. I was willing to trust Him. I was at the end of myself. If this didn't work, I knew nothing else will.

I remember the pastor doing an altar call. I went to the altar and fell on my knees and begin to pray. I asked God to take away ALL the HURT and ALL the PAIN. I was tired of carrying it. I didn't care who was looking at me, I just wanted to be FREE. They sang a song in church, "Take your burdens to the Lord and leave them there." And that's exactly what I did.

Everything I learned as a child came to mind as I kneeled at the altar. My eyes opened spiritually and I was able to start the process of healing. The Altar was the beginning of my healing and the start to my road map of deliverance.

Rejected from the womb, accepted by God was my reality. I learned how to let God heal me and love me properly. It was a PROCESS. It was MY process. It was a JOURNEY. It was MY journey. It is my REALITY!!! I lived the good and bad. Now my life is better.

I lived many years feeling rejected. I am now free from it. I no longer allow it to hold me down, hold me back and paralyze me from moving forward in life. I wanted to share with you my life story, and how God healed me so that you can know it's possible for you to begin your healing process, too.

If you experience rejection and abandonment from a parent, I want to encourage you to seek God and allow Him to heal you as you learn to find your identity.

Your life will NOW become better. You will feel refreshed, renewed, excited about your life and enjoy this new journey. You will be able to face and embrace rejections. It will no longer be your identity. You will learn how to use rejection from your past as a learning experience and it will NEVER hold you hostage again. You will no longer be a prisoner, but you will be a free man/woman because you are accepted by God.

Get ready to explore the journey. Get ready for your freedom and get ready to finally receive acceptance. You deserve it!

Connect with LiQuiche

Email: Acceptedbygod2018@gmail.com

Facebook: LiQuiche Young

Acknowledgements

I would like to thank every person that's entered my life. Some people were seasonal and others were a lifetime. Thank you to my grandmother for loving me and raising. Thank you to the many pastors that has taught me about God and having faith. A special thanks to my stepfather and my God parents for always being there when I needed you. Lastly I'm thanks for test and my testimony. I'm thankful that I'm accepted by God.